MARVIN TERBAN

Your FOOT'S on My FEET!

And Other Tricky Nouns

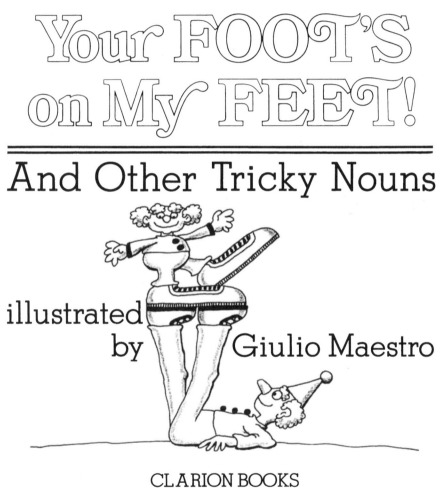

illustrated by Giulio Maestro

CLARION BOOKS
NEW YORK

Clarion Books
a Houghton Mifflin Company imprint
215 Park Avenue South, New York, NY 10003
Text copyright © 1986 by Marvin Terban
Illustration copyright © 1986 by Giulio Maestro
First Clarion paperback edition, 1987; reissued, 2007.

For information about permission to reproduce selections from this book,
write to trade.permissions @ hmhco.com or to Permissions, Houghton Mifflin
Harcourt Publishing Company, 3 Park Avenue, 19th Floor, New York, New York
10016

www.clarionbooks.com

Printed in the U.S.A.

The Library of Congress has cataloged the original hardcover edition as follows:

Terban, Marvin.
Your foot's on my feet!
Summary: Explores the plural of 90 irregular
nouns such as mouse/mice in humorous rhymes
and tongue twisters.
0-89919-411-7   0-89919-413-3 (pa)
1. English language—Nouns—Juvenile literature.
2. English language—Number—Juvenile literature.
[1. English language—Noun. 2. English language—Number]
I. Maestro, Giulio, ill.   II. Title.
PE1216.T47   1986   428.2   85-19561
PA ISBN-13: 978-0-618-19166-6   PA ISBN-10: 0-618-19166-6

EB 10 9 8 7 6 5 4
4500602154

For my daughter Jennifer
There's no plural for you
because you're one of a kind.

Contents

Introduction

English is a tricky language. Many words don't follow regular rules. Take nouns, for instance. A noun is a word that names

a person   **teacher**

a place   **house**

or a thing.   **pencil**

If a noun names two or more

persons   **teachers**

places   **houses**

or things   **pencils**

we call it a *plural* noun. As you can see, to make a noun plural you usually just add *s*.

Usually, but *not always.*

Only regular nouns add *s.* Irregular ones don't.
Some irregular nouns have new endings:

country   **countries**

Some irregular nouns change their spellings in
the middle:

foot   **feet**

Some irregular nouns don't change at all:

sheep   **sheep**

And some even have more than one plural.

octopus   **octopuses**   and   **octopi**

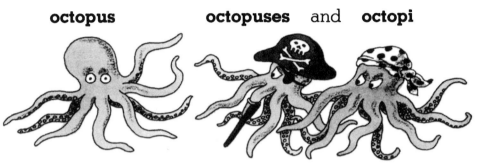

Plural nouns are often peculiar because so many words in English come from foreign languages. That's why one **chateau** becomes two **chateaux.**

And one **madame** becomes two **mesdames.**

These words are from French. Some words in this book come from Greek, Latin, and other languages.

The tongue-twisting verses and comical pictures in the pages that follow will help you learn all of the common irregular plural nouns in English.

Nouns That Change Their Endings

One **boy** + one **boy** = two **boys.**

A **girl** and another **girl** are two **girls.**

Girl and **boy** are regular nouns. They just add *s* when they're more than one.

But when one **child** plays with another **child,**

there are two **children** playing.

Three new letters, r-e-n, are added to the end of the word child to make the word plural. Children is an irregular noun. There are many more irregular nouns that add new endings or change their old endings. Here are some of the most common.

Obnoxious **ox**
unlocks
the box.

And the **oxen**
put rocks in
the socks of
the fox!

Wild woolly **Wolf** met Ms. Hood in the wood.
Ms. Hood understood that most **wolves**
mean no good (in all likelihood).

On the edge of a **shelf**
sits an **elf** by himself.

On the elephant's **shelves**
there is no room for **elves.**

The **thief** stole the beef that was briefly at Steve's.
No one believes what is told him by **thieves.**

A fly
tried to buy
just one **die**
from some mice.

Then for twice
that one price
bought a nice
pair of **dice.**

"Good grief!" cried the **leaf** as it flew from the tree.
The **leaves** on Eve's sleeves don't look pleasing to me.

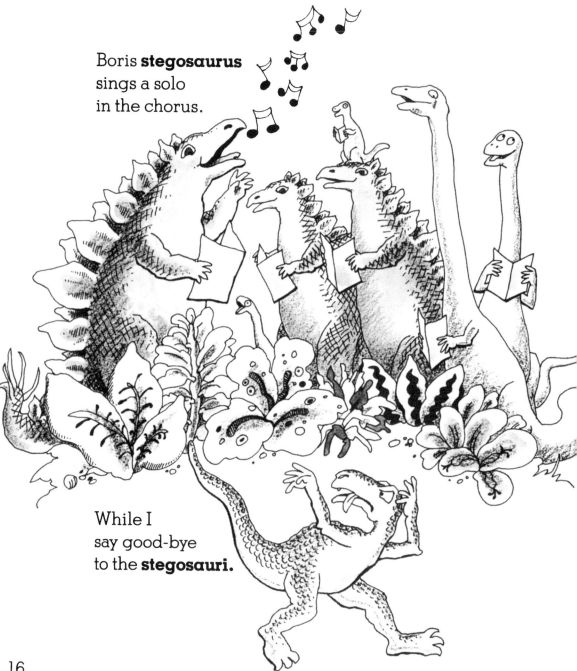

Boris **stegosaurus**
sings a solo
in the chorus.

While I
say good-bye
to the **stegosauri.**

The mild crocodile always smiled at the **child**.

The **children** went wild on the isle in the Nile.

The giraffe on the raft thought the **calf** was half daft.
All the comical **calves** and the crazy cow laughed.

A **lady** bathes her **baby**
   in the shady babbling brook.

The **ladies** and their **babies**
   are just learning how to cook.

Ted
fed
Fred
a little **loaf**
of bread.

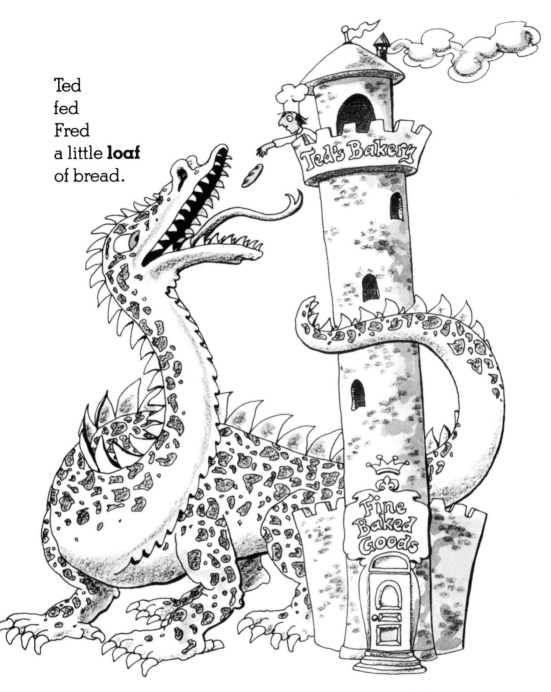

Fred said, "Ted, I'd like larger **loaves** instead!"

A **woman** in a wig watched a walrus dance the jig.
The **women** in the window wished
   the pig were not so big.

Columbus met an **alumnus**
   of a Spanish sailing college
and enlightened the **alumni**
   when he showed off all his knowledge.

alumna   **alumnae**

Photograph of **half** a giraffe.

Photographs of **halves** of giraffes.

datum

Fact

1. There is only one fact on this page.

data

FACTS
EVERY FACT YOU EVER WANTED TO KNOW... AND SOME YOU DIDN'T

This **fez** is fuzzier than those **fezzes.**

"Create a **tomato!** Inflate a **potato!**"

She ate those **tomatoes** and plates of **potatoes.**

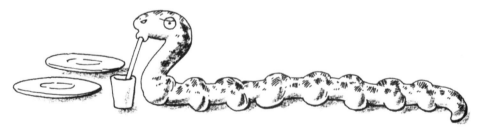

sheaf

sheaves

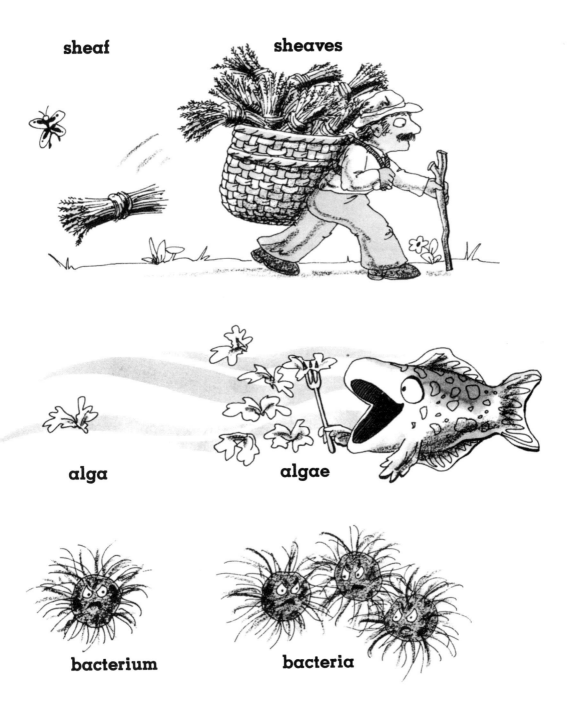

alga

algae

bacterium

bacteria

crisis crises

Berry
on **belly**
of **baby**
in **buggy**

Berries, bellies, babies, buggies

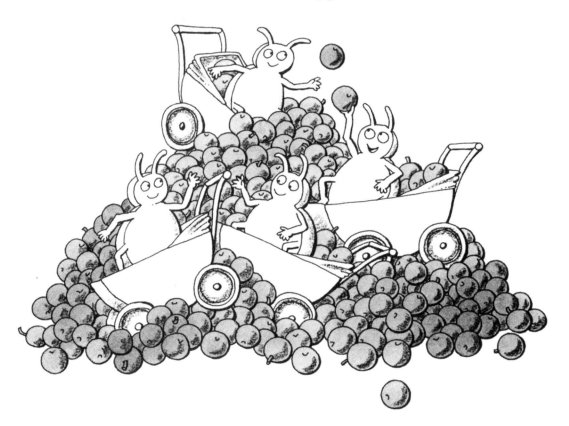

When Muppy, my **puppy**,
fell in the cup he
upset all the **puppies.**

My **guppy** had **guppies.**

MOM OF THE YEAR!

As you can see, when there's a consonant before the final y, you change the y to i and add es. But don't do this if the noun is a proper noun (one that names a specific person, place, or thing). Here are two examples:

There is an East **Germany** and a West **Germany.** That makes two **Germanys.**

Last year I had one **Mary** in my class. This year I have three **Marys.**

Nouns That Change
in the Middle

Sometimes the noun changes its spelling right in the middle.

If one **tooth** falls out, you still have plenty of **teeth** left.

Here are more irregular nouns that change in the middle when they become plural.

My Mountie's **mouse** mounts mounds of ice.
My mother makes music with my merry **mice.**

My spouse says, "A **louse** in the house isn't nice.
But lousier still is to have lots of **lice.**"

Willy's **wife** Wilma will wiggle her eyes.

Five lively **wives** tried to fly through the skies.

A **knife** and a spoon will soon zoom to the moon.

Two **knives** and a fork took a bus to New York.

My **goose** is loose!
Police! Police!
Maurice had no peace
and released all the **geese.**

Jogger the frog flexed his **foot** on the street.
Pete parakeet had a fleet pair of **feet.**

"Tell me the truth! Where is Ruth's **tooth?**"
"I hid all the **teeth** beneath the red wreath."

The **man** with the pen
wrote a poem to the hen.

The **men** had a yen
to be children again.

When you read you may see lots of words that end with **man** or **men** such as:

caveman / cavemen	fisherman / fishermen
policeman / policemen	fireman / firemen
mailman / mailmen	gentleman / gentlemen
chairman / chairmen	clergyman / clergymen
marksman / marksmen	coachman / coachmen
serviceman / servicemen	tribesman / tribesmen
workman / workmen	townsman / townsmen

But nowadays many people prefer to use words that don't have **man** or **men** at the end. Since both a man or a woman can work for the police department, put out fires, head a committee, and deliver mail, we call them police officers, fire fighters, chairpersons, and mail carriers. Signs that used to say Men Working are being changed to People Working. These changes in the language show that both men and women can have the same jobs.

Years ago, a warship was sometimes called a *man-of-war*. Its plural would never change to *people-of-war*. If you saw two of these ships, they were *men-of-war*. There are some other words that end with man that have nothing to do with male persons. They just add s to make their plurals:

A **talisman** on an **ottoman**.
Two **talismans** on two **ottomans**.

My **mother-in-law** saw the macaw draw its claw.
The **mothers-in-law** found a flaw in the straw.

brother-in-law	**brothers-in-law**
sister-in-law	**sisters-in-law**
mother-in-law	**mothers-in-law**
father-in-law	**fathers-in-law**

Nouns That
Don't Change at All

Some nouns stay exactly the same in both the singular and plural. One **moose** plus ninety-nine more are a hundred **moose.** They're not mooses and they're not meese! They're moose. This chapter will show you other nouns that don't change.

Dora's dear **deer** was so full of good cheer
that she naturally had many friends who were **deer.**

steep,
was
that
hill
a
up
jeep
a
drove
sheep
a
When

he woke up the **sheep** who were deeply asleep.

A silly **swine**
sent a valentine
to a porcupine.

It's not so fine
to wine and dine
with ninety-nine **swine.**

A **bison**
put spice in
the salad and stew.

Two **bison**
threw dice in
the game at the zoo.

I missed the World **Series** in 1904,
but I've seen many **series** and hope to see more.

My moody **moose** Bruce
spilled all of his juice.

Under the moon
the cow moos at the **moose.**

Nouns That Have More Than One Plural

Some nouns can't make up their minds what their plurals should be and so they have two of them. One irregular noun has three. Why? Because that's just the way the English language developed over hundreds of years.

For instance, if you see a whole bunch of shiny things with fins swimming by you in the ocean, you can call them

millions of **fish** or millions of **fishes.**
Some other nouns with two or more plurals are in this chapter.

Hippopotamus wonders just what all the fuss is.
They're **hippopotami** or **hippopotamuses.**

Octopus bakes a pie for the other **octopi.**

Octopuses are **octopi.**
Whatever you call them, let them swim by.

halo

halos or **haloes**

appendix

appendixes or **appendices**

BOOK-WORMS UNITE!

antenna

bug **antennae**   tv **antennas**

a **dwarf** on a **wharf**

seven **dwarfs** on seven **wharfs**

seven **dwarves** on seven **wharves**

The noun **staff** has different plurals depending on what it means.

staff #1.
Plural: **staves**

staff #2.
Plural: **staves**

staff #3.
Plural: **staffs**

Take *this* **scarf**
and *that* scarf
and *this* one
and *that*.

And *these* **scarves**
and *those* **scarfs.**
But not that cravat!

Gus on the **bus** wonders, "One *s* or two?"
Buses or **busses** — both spellings will do!

The team's score is **zero.**
These guys are not heroes,
and they keep on adding more **zeros** to **zeroes.**

"No one can stop a **volcano** from popping."

"Volcanos! Volcanoes! Stuff's dropping! Start mopping!"

The **cactus** attacked us.
It whacked us and smacked us.

As a matter of fact, I
don't like any **cacti.**
(P.S. I don't like **cactuses** either!)

a **hoof**	**hoofs**	or	**hooves**
on a	on		on
roof	**roofs**		**roofs**

Animals With More
Than One Plural

Oh, give me a home where the **buffalo** roam...

Oh, give me a home where the **buffalos** roam...

Oh, give me a home where the **buffaloes** roam...

And the **deer** and the **antelope** play.

mink / mink or minks
    okapi / okapi or okapis

quail / quail or quails
grouse / grouse or grouses
    platypus / platypuses or platypi

wallaby / wallaby or wallabies
weasel / weasel or weasels

zebra / zebra or zebras
antelope / antelope or antelopes
rhinoceros / rhinoceros or rhinoceroses

tarantula / tarantulas or tarantulae
panther / panther or panthers
otter / otter or otters
turkey / turkey or turkeys

hare / hare or hares
hart / hart or harts
   ibex / ibex or ibexes

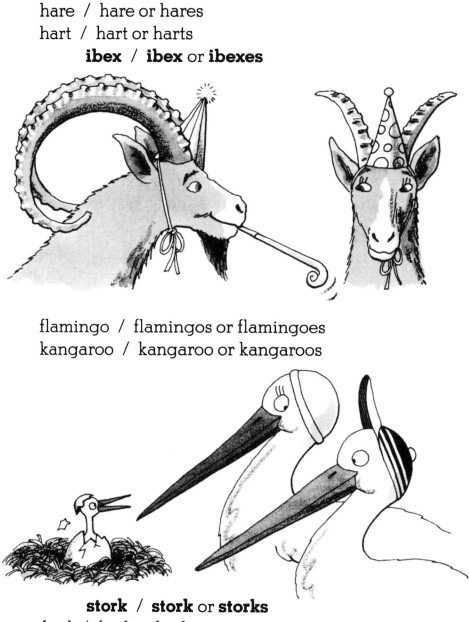

flamingo / flamingos or flamingoes
kangaroo / kangaroo or kangaroos

   stork / stork or storks
fowl / fowl or fowls

Fish and Sea Mammals With More Than One Plural

The plural is the same as the singular or adds *s* or *es*.

This fabulous **fish** always knows what my wish is:
A dish of **fish** and dishes of **fishes**.

squid / squid or squids
halibut / halibut or halibuts
marlin / marlin or marlins
trout / trout or trouts
sardine / sardine or sardines
tuna / tuna or tunas
tarpon / tarpon or tarpons

whale / whale or whales
perch / perch or perches
bass / bass or basses
walrus / walrus or walruses

grouper / **grouper** or **groupers**
haddock / haddock or haddocks

herring / **herring** or **herrings**
pickerel / pickerel or pickerels

salmon / salmon or salmons
sturgeon / **sturgeon** or **sturgeons**

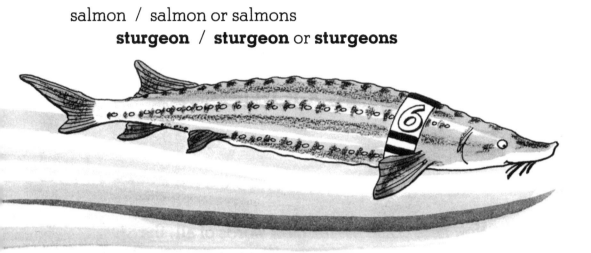

shad / shad or shads
mullet / mullet or mullets
porpoise / porpoise or porpoises
cod / cod or cods
hake / **hake** or **hakes**

·5·

Odditties

Now here come the trickiest words of all, the irregular irregular nouns. These are the really weird ones. Some plural nouns have no singulars. Some plurals are spelled exactly the same as the singulars but are pronounced very differently. English is peculiar, isn't it?

1. Plural nouns that have no singulars

suds

Also:

pliers
pants
overalls
numismatics
arms
cattle
bellows

chaps

archives
athletics
alms
boondocks
funnies
blue jeans

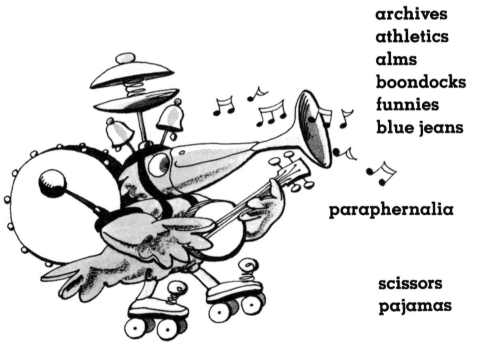

paraphernalia

scissors
pajamas

2. The singular and plural of the following nouns are spelled the same, but they are pronounced differently.

chassis (shas' ē) **chassis** (shas' ēz)

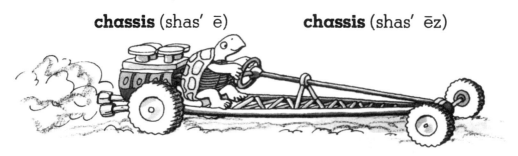

corps (kôr) **corps** (kôrz)

chamois (sham' ē) **chamois** (sham' ēz)

3. And just when you thought you understood these tricky irregular plurals...

goose **geese**

mongoose **mongooses**

As you can see, there are many ways to make plurals of irregular words, but what about numbers and letters? How would you say that you had more than one *j* in your name? How would you say that your phone number had more than one *6* in it? Easy! To make numbers and letters plural just add *'s*. Here are some examples:

I spell my name with four **j's.**

My phone number has six **6's** in it.

You spell **Mississippi** with four **s's,** two **p's,** and four **i's.**

Here is an alphabetical list of the irregular nouns featured in this book.

Pages	Singular	Plural
23	alga	algae
55		alms
20	alumna	alumnae
20	alumnus	alumni
41	antenna	antennas/antennae
41	appendix	appendixes/appendices
55		archives
55		arms
55		athletics
18, 24	baby	babies
23	bacterium	bacteria
24	belly	bellies
55		bellows
24	berry	berries
36	bison	bison
55		blue jeans
55		boondocks
32	brother-in-law	brothers-in-law
47	buffalo	buffalos/buffaloes/buffalo
24	buggy	buggies
44	bus	buses/busses
46	cactus	cacti/cactuses
18	calf	calves

Pages	Singular	Plural
55		cattle
56	chamois	chamois
55		chaps
56	chassis	chassis
9	chateau	chateaux
12, 17	child	children
56	corps	corps
8	country	countries
24	crisis	crises
21	datum	data
33	deer	deer
15	die	dice
42	dwarf	dwarfs/dwarves
14	elf	elves
32	father-in-law	fathers-in-law
8, 30	foot	feet
22	fez	fezzes
38, 51	fish	fish/fishes
55		funnies
26	Germany	Germanys
29	goose	geese
25	guppy	guppies
21	half	halves
41	halo	halos/haloes
39	hippopotamus	hippopotami/hippopotamuses
47	hoof	hoofs/hooves
29	knife	knives

Pages	Singular	Plural
18	lady	ladies
16	leaf	leaves
19	loaf	loaves
28	louse	lice
9	madame	mesdames
30, 31	man	men
26	Mary	Marys
56	mongoose	mongoose
33, 37	moose	moose
32	mother-in-law	mothers-in-law
27	mouse	mice
55		numismatics
9, 40	octopus	octopi/octopuses
32	ottoman	ottomans
55		overalls
13	ox	oxen
55		pajamas
55		pants
55		paraphernalia
55		pliers
22	potato	potatoes
25	puppy	puppies
44	scarf	scarves/scarfs
55		scissors
36	series	series
23	sheaf	sheaves

Pages	Singular	Plural
8, 34	sheep	sheep
14	shelf	shelves
32	sister-in-law	sisters-in-law
43	staff	staves/staffs
16	stegosaurus	stegosauri
54		suds
35	swine	swine
32	talisman	talismans
27, 30	tooth	teeth
15	thief	thieves
22	tomato	tomatoes
45	volcano	volcanos/volcanoes
42	wharf	wharfs/wharves
28	wife	wives
13	wolf	wolves
20	woman	women
45	zero	zeros/zeroes

ABOUT THE AUTHOR

Your Foot's on My Feet is Marvin Terban's fifth word play book for Clarion. Mr. Terban teaches at Columbia Grammar and Preparatory School in Manhattan where he delights his students by finding new ways to teach English. He also directs children's plays during the summer at Cejwin Camps in Port Jervis, New York. Mr. Terban lives in New York City with his wife Karen, a teacher, their two children, and a cat.

ABOUT THE ARTIST

Giulio Maestro has illustrated many books for children including five by Marvin Terban. He has also written and illustrated three riddle books of his own for Clarion. Mr. Maestro lives in Madison, Connecticut, with his wife Betsy, a writer, and their two children.